942.05

# The Reign
## of
# Philip and Mary

### by
### David Loades

Published by  The Davenant Press
              21, Beaumont Street
              Oxford OX1 2NH
              England

Printed by Parchment (Oxford) Limited

ISBN 1 85944 205 6

The Reign of Philip and Mary

This is the first edition of a title commissioned
by Headstart History Publishing as part of the
Headstart History Papers


A CIP catalogue record for this book is available from the
British Library

Contents

## Biographical Note

David Loades was born in Cambridge in 1934 and educated at the Perse School and Emmanuel College, Cambridge where he gained BA in 1958, Ph.D. in 1961 and D. Litt. in 1981. He was awarded the Prince Consort Prize and Seeley Medal in 1961 for his work on Tudor conspiracies. He was Lecturer at the University of St. Andrews from 1961-3, Lecturer (1963-70), Senior Lecturer (1970-7), Reader (1977-80) at the University of Durham and Professor of History at the University of Wales. Bangor (1980-1995). He was Visiting Fellow, All Souls College, Oxford, 1988-9, Vice-Chancellor's Visiting Fellow, New Zealand, 1993 and has been Honorary Research Professor at the University of Sheffield since 1996. He was elected Fellow of the Royal Historical Society in 1967 and FSA in 1983. He has written extensively on the Tudors and in particular on the mid-Tudor period as well as on the Tudor Navy and on the English Reformation. He has recently co-edited *The Anthony Roll of Henry VIII's Navy* with Charles Knighton and amongst other things is currently writing a biography of the young Elizabeth.

He is Director of the British Academy John Foxe Project which was established in 1993 to produce the definitive edition of the *Acts and Monuments of John Foxe*

# Introduction

Until comparatively recently Mary's historical reputation followed the lines laid down by John Foxe a few years after her death.

'...we shall find never no reign of any prince in this land, or any other, which had ever to shew in it (for the proportion of time) so many arguments of God's great wrath and displeasure as was to be seen in the reign of this Queen Mary, whether we behold the shortness of her time, or the unfortunate event of all her purposes. Who seemed never to purpose anything which came luckily to pass, neither did anything serve to her purpose, whatsoever she took in hand touching her own private affairs.' [1]

Foxe never claimed that she was anything other than a lawful Queen, and the husband she chose to marry a lawful king; nor were they evil in themselves. They were, he believed, an affliction imposed upon England by God for his own purposes. Mary, in particular, was the victim of a clerical conspiracy to reimpose the control of idolatry and superstition. Like Judas Iscariot, she was destined to do what she did do, but was not thereby absolved from responsibility. God brought her to misfortune for his own glory and the future well being of England.

Catholic scholars, who had no time for Foxe's providentialism, and believed that Mary's purposes had been good in themselves, could not avoid the fact of her failure, which they were inclined to blame upon a mistaken marriage. Some have seen her life as a romantic tragedy, in which the hapless woman has loomed larger than the frustrated politician. Nowadays analysts of her reign have abandoned both denominational and romantic agendas, and opinion is broadly divided into two schools. On the one hand are those who believe that she was a skilful ruler pursuing sensible policies, and was defeated simply because she died before she could bring them to fruition. On the other are those who argue that she was inept, and that her policies carried the seeds of their own frustration. They would have failed anyway, even if she had lived longer. Most of the questions which may confront the modern student of her reign are shaped by this conflict of interpretation. Was Mary's marriage a mistake? Was Philip a help or a hindrance to her? Would her religious policy have succeeded in time? Was the persecution a mistaken strategy?

In confronting such questions, it is a mistake to assume that the most recent 'revisionist' argument is always correct. Revisionist historians are normally trying to correct what they see as distortions in accepted views rather than to present a balanced synthesis. Eventually the reader must decide, but a polemical attitude is seldom helpful. Nor should the reign be approached through modern secular and democratic prejudices. Popular support was not crucial to sixteenth century governments, and should not be used as a yardstick of legitimacy. Everyone believed that there was one true interpretation of the Christian faith, and that error spelt ruin, not only for the individual but also for the realm.

# I
## The making of a Queen

Mary was born at Greenwich on the 18th February 1516 to Catherine, the queen of Henry VIII. Her parentage was to determine the whole course of her life, and consequently her story really begins several years earlier. Henry was the only surviving son of his father, King Henry VII, and in spite of his family name was about 75% English by blood. [2] Catherine was the third daughter of Ferdinand of Aragon and Isabella of Castille, and was consequently 100% Spanish by blood. She had come to England in 1501, after a protracted negotiation, as the bride of Henry VII's eldest son, Arthur, Prince of Wales. Arthur died in 1502, and Catherine's mother, Isabella, in 1503. For a variety of reasons both Henry and Ferdinand wanted Catherine to stay in England, and there was talk of her marrying Henry's second son, the Duke of York. Both sides blew hot and cold about the negotiation, and nothing was concluded. Catherine remained in an uncomfortable limbo, and convinced herself that God intended her to marry the younger Henry. Consequently, when Henry VIII declared this intention within weeks of his father's death in 1509, she believed that he was acting directly upon divine inspiration. Meanwhile her elder sister, Juana, had married Philip of Burgundy, the only son of the Emperor Maximilian, and had born him two sons, Charles and Ferdinand. Philip died young in 1506, and his elder son succeeded him as Archduke. Taking advantage of Juana's absence, and of her uncertain mental condition, Ferdinand of Aragon had secured control of Castille after Isabella's death, and consequently after 1506 his grandson Charles of Burgundy was the direct heir to both the Crowns of Spain.

There were always doubts about Henry VIII's marriage to his brother's widow. Such a marriage was forbidden by canon law, but Julius II had dispensed the canonical impediment at the end of 1503. For most people (including Henry and Catherine) that was sufficient, but doubts lingered. Was the impediment simply one of canon law, or was it one of Divine Law; and if the latter, could the pope dispense it? None of this mattered at the time, and at first the relationship was a great success. However, Catherine miscarried of a daughter at the beginning of 1510, and their son born early in 1511 lived only a few weeks. In 1515 another son was born prematurely and dead, and the king began to have qualms. Catherine was more than a child bearer, she was a highly intelligent councillor and support, but she was also committed to her father's cause, and Henry and Ferdinand had fallen out. In 1515 the king was beginning to rethink his position. However, in 1516 two things happened. In February Mary was born, alive and flourishing, and shortly after Ferdinand died to be succeeded by the sixteen year old Charles. Although Catherine soon became as devoted to her nephew as she had been to her father, her marriage appeared to have been redeemed. Henry referred to Mary as a 'token of hope'. Within days of her birth she was established with the lavish household of a royal princess, and was recognised as her father's heir, but that did not correspond with the king's real intention.

Henry had no desire to leave his crown to a woman, and in England there was no Salic Law to prevent that from happening. [3] There were valid reasons for this, because no woman had ever made good a claim to the English crown, and the position was consequently unprecedented. By the normal laws of inheritance a woman's property passed to her husband in full ownership on marriage, and nobody knew whether this applied to the crown or not. The precedents of both Brittany and Castile suggested that the realm would pass into foreign control, unless the queen married one of her own subjects, which would be a prescription for civil strife.

As long as there was a prospect of Catherine bearing a son, the king pushed these worries to the back of his mind, but in 1518 she miscarried again, and there were no further conceptions. Henry did not act precipitately, but in 1519 his mistress, Elizabeth Blount, bore him a healthy son and this convinced him (if he needed convincing) that his lack of a lawful heir was all Catherine's fault. With the succession gnawing at his conscience, in 1525 he set up the nine year old Mary with her own council at Ludlow, in nominal control of the marches of Wales; and at the same time created his six year old illegitimate son Henry Fitzroy, Duke of Richmond and sent him to the north of England with a similar council. These actions, which were clearly taken on the advice, and possibly the initiative, of Cardinal Wolsey, sent out an ambiguous message. In spite of her grand train and theoretical responsibilities, Mary was not created Princess of Wales, which would have been an explicit recognition of her status as heir. At the same time the Duchy of Richmond was a royal title.

Until this time, Mary had lived the orthodox life of a royal princess. She was surrounded by ceremony and deference, and her education in piety, music, Latin and needlework had begun almost as soon as she could toddle. She was unusually close to both her parents, and her father delighted to show her off at court. Contrary to what is sometimes alleged, she was not tutored by Juan Luis Vives, although he did provide Catherine with an advanced manual for her instruction. [4] Her tutors were lesser, but competent men, and she does not seem to have shown any great precocity, except, perhaps in music. She was on the marriage market almost from birth, but the only serious negotiation was for the hand of her cousin, Charles, already king of Spain and from 1519 Holy Roman Emperor. In 1522 he visited England and they met. The young man professed to be charmed by the six year old, but his motives were political, and it was never likely that he would be prepared to wait for her to grow up. Mary remembered her solemn suitor for the rest of her life, and although they never met again, his influence over her was to become of the greatest importance. Henry had negotiated with Charles on the understanding that Mary was his heir, but by 1525 when the latter repudiated the agreement, that was becoming less clear. Allegedly it was a similar negotiation with Francis I of France which first raised the question of the princess's legitimacy, but that was a mere pretext to explore the king's own doubts. By 1525 it was clear that Catherine would not conceive again, and Henry had three options: he could leave the situation as it was, accepting the problems to come; he could seek to legitimise the Duke of Richmond, and bypass Mary; or he could repudiate Catherine and start again. The second was too hazardous and complicated to be taken seriously, and the first really necessitated an early marriage for Mary in the hope that she would solve the problems by bearing a son in her father's lifetime. However, even at nine it was clear that Mary was a slow developer, physically, and it would be at least another six years before she was ready for co-habitation. Henry was understandably impatient, and it was the third option that he decided upon. This was nothing to do with the charms of Anne Boleyn, who only appeared on the scene after the decision was made.

Having made his decision, Henry handled what was bound to be an emotionally and politically sensitive issue with total ineptitude. Tactfully approached, Catherine might have accepted that it was her duty to retire gracefully into a nunnery. As it was she was outraged, and determined to defend her position by every resource at her command. Henry had had the temerity to suggest that their union had offended the laws of God, whereas she knew that God had specifically arranged the marriage in answer to her prayers. The tortuous and momentous politics of the next eight years need not concern us here. Mary remained at Ludlow, largely ignorant of the storms brewing, until 1529. When she was recalled, aged thirteen, her father was already deep in his affair with Anne Boleyn, and fighting a futile and frustrating battle with both the Pope and the Emperor for an annulment. Mary instinctively and passionately sided with her mother, and relations with her father became increasingly strained and difficult. It was probably the tension of this situation, combined with a slightly delayed puberty, which gave her the menstrual problems which were to remain almost to the end of her life. Henry sent his physicians to care for her frequent illnesses, but was unrelenting in other ways, because he could ill afford to be otherwise. Finally, in 1533 he cut the Gordian knot. Cranmer pronounced his first marriage unlawful, and he married Anne Boleyn, defying the anathemas which promptly arrived from Rome, the hostility of the Emperor, and the deep unease of many of his own subjects. Catherine was declared to be Princess Dowager of Wales, and Mary illegitimate.

Although Eustace Chapuys, the Emperor's ambassador, claimed otherwise, and did his utmost to stir up resistance, Catherine's demotion was not callously handled; she was properly provided for. [5] It was Mary who received the rough end of her father's displeasure. She was now seventeen, and had all the obstinacy of both her parents. She refused to accept either her mother's dishonour or her own, embroidering her rejection with hysterical outbursts. In consequence her household was disbanded, and she was sent under virtual house arrest, into the household which had just been created for the young princess Elizabeth, born in September 1533. Henry forbade her to communicate with her mother, a prohibition which loyal servants enabled them to avoid, and tried to keep Chapuy's servants away from her. Given the widespread disquiet in the country at this turn of events, Mary represented a much greater threat to her father than Catherine did, because her inexperience and wounded feelings made her much more open to manipulation. At the same time, Mary convinced herself that it was Anne Boleyn who was to blame for all the humiliations which she endured, and vented her feelings whenever possible. Catherine died in January 1536 and Mary, who had not been allowed to see her, felt the blow keenly. It did not, however, alter her attitude, and when Anne Boleyn suddenly fell from grace and was executed in May 1536, she was convinced that her troubles were over. It was with astonishment and alarm that she became disabused over the next three months. Her father intended to persist with his ecclesiastical supremacy, and she would continue to be illegitimate. After holding out for an agonising month under threat of execution for high treason, and wracked with stress related illness, in July she capitulated and accepted the situation which Henry had decreed.

Within a few weeks her household was restored, and she was back at court, on friendly terms with the new Queen, Jane Seymour, and apparently reconciled to her father. No one knew, or now knows, whether her submission was feigned or real, and perhaps she hardly knew herself. The birth of Prince Edward in 1537 took some of the pressure off her, and she was very careful to give no countenance to any opposition, even if it invoked her name. Apart from the fact that there were no further marriage negotiations (or at least not serious ones) her life as a royal lady was resumed. Although she remained illegitimate, in 1543 she was restored to the order of succession, after Edward, but ahead of Elizabeth. [6] Much of her time was occupied with renewed study in the humanist manner, and she enjoyed friendly relations with Catherine Parr, her father's last wife, who was not much older than herself. When Henry died in January 1547, the Emperor at first withheld recognition from Edward VI on the grounds that Mary was the late king's only legitimate child. She, however, made no move to challenge her brother, either because she recognised his legitimacy or because she realised that such a challenge would be futile. Until this time, although Mary had her own household and favoured residences, she had no property of her own. Henry's will belatedly rectified that situation, bestowing upon her an estate worth more than £3000 a year, mainly in East Anglia. These lands had recently been forfeited by the Duke of Norfolk, attainted in 1546, and they carried with them the well developed Howard affinity. Mary withdrew from the court, and spent the next five years building up her following, and converting this affinity to her own use.

Mary's relations with her brother's regents (Edward was nine in 1547) were dominated by the question of religion. As soon the Duke of Somerset, who was Lord Protector from 1547 to 1549, began to move the church in a protestant direction, the princess objected. She did this, not on the ground that protestantism was heresy, but that her father's settlement must not be disturbed until Edward assumed the Supremacy at full age. She rejected the council's argument that it was entitled to exercise that authority on his behalf. This was potentially dangerous, as she represented a strong body of opinion, and remorseless pressure was applied to her, particularly by Somerset's successor, the Earl of Warwick. [7] Edward, who was emerging as a committed protestant, approved of this pressure, and his relations with his sister cooled. Mary was more concerned to protect her own conscience and enjoy the traditional rites than to challenge the government, and never made any move of overt resistance, but she refused conformity. In this she was strongly encouraged by the ambassadors and other envoys of Charles V, and again regarded the Emperor as a protector and

4

father figure, as she had during her earlier troubles between 1533 and 1536. In the summer of 1550 she was so desperate to avoid the pressure upon her that a plot was hatched to spirit her away to Flanders, but at the last minute either her nerve failed or wiser councils prevailed, and she stayed in England, her tensions with the council unresolved. Charles nevertheless made it clear that further pressure would lead to a diplomatic breach, and the deadlock remained.

Consequently, when Edward became ill in the spring of 1553, Mary was the acknowledged champion of 'the old faith' as represented by Henry VIII's curious compromise, a powerful magnate in her own right, and the heir to the throne both by the statute of 1543, and by her father's will.

## II
## The succession crisis and the forming of a government

Just how and when the plot was developed to exclude Mary from the succession is not clear. It used to be believed that it was the culmination of a long matured scheme by the Earl of Warwick, now Duke of Northumberland, to bring the Crown into his own family. According to this interpretation, he intrigued to match the protestant claimant, Lady Jane Grey, with his only unmarried son, and persuaded or bullied the sick king into accepting this arrangement by pointing out that Mary would certainly undo the Godly reformation by which he set such store. After the plot had failed this was a neat and convenient way of disposing of the responsibility, by placing all the blame upon a man whom nobody liked, and who was in any case destined for an early traitor's death. So after the event everyone agreed that it had been all Northumberland's fault, and they all remembered thinking so at the time!

However, the truth was much less simple. Edward had begun to think about the succession before he was ill, and certainly before it acquired any sort of urgency. Probably about the beginning of the year 1553 he had jotted down some of these thoughts in a 'Device for the succession'. At that point he had three concerns, gender, legitimacy and religion. Like his father, he was determined that the crown must pass to a male, legitimately born into a legitimate line. Of course the problem only arose if he left no son of his own, so he bypassed that possibility, not because he knew it would not happen but because it did not create an issue. His cousin Mary Stuart was undoubtedly legitimate, but she was well below the marriageable age, was committed in France, and his father had ignored her. [8] Edward did the same. Both his half sisters were of marriageable age, and might well have sons in due course, but both were illegitimate, so he ignored them as well. That brought him to his cousin Frances Grey, Duchess of Suffolk, the daughter of his aunt Mary and Charles Brandon. Because she was female, he set her aside as well, and started with any son who might be born to her. This was highly speculative as her daughters were adolescents and she had not conceived for years. He then proceeded to any sons who might be born to her daughters. Should he die before any of this had happened, the crown was to be placed in abeyance, with Frances as protector until one of her daughters performed the magic feat! This was not serious politics, and it does not appear that anyone knew about it (not even Northumberland) until much later.

During the spring of 1553 Edward became seriously ill, but it was an illness with remissions, and as late as the beginning of June some optimists were still forecasting a complete recovery. Meanwhile Northumberland, having failed in a long quest after a daughter of the Earl of Cumberland, settled upon Jane Grey for his son Guildford, more because her father was amenable than because she was close to the crown. At the time of the wedding in May, it was merely noted by observers that the bride was related to the king. In early June, however, events began to move very fast. Edward suddenly became much worse, and his physicians, so recently optimistic, started

5

to say that his death was not only inevitable, but imminent. Edward remembered his Device, and probably showed it to the Duke. As it stood it was useless, with all its dependence upon unborn sons, nor was the protectorship proposal realistic. If Mary and Elizabeth were to be excluded, and no male available, the logical heir was Frances Grey herself. Neither Edward nor Northumberland wanted her, probably for different reasons. However by altering 'the heirs male of the Lady Jane' to 'the Lady Jane and her heirs male', a solution could be arrived at which suited both the conspiritors. Edward liked Jane, and approved of her piety. If a woman had got to succeed, better her than any other. For Northumberland, the prospect of his daughter in law as queen was even more attractive; especially as he knew that Mary, the heir by law, heartily detested him. So the plot was cobbled together; a desperate improvisation with neither logic nor law to commend it.

The assumption that the initiative was the Duke's cannot be proved, and the 'Device' suggests that the idea had been in Edward's mind for some time. What is reasonably certain is that Northumberland did nothing to dissuade the king, embraced the idea warmly, and did his best to promote it. The Council and Law Officers were aghast. Henry's statute was unrepealed, and it was by no means certain that, as a minor, Edward could even make a valid will, let alone dispose of the Crown in this cavalier manner. The king charged them upon their allegiance to convert his Device into a valid will, and they had no choice but to submit. Not only was he their lawful king, but in spite of his youth and sickness, he was also a Tudor and determined to be obeyed. What they appear to have produced was not a will, but Letters Patent, dated 21st June, and settling the succession in accordance with the king's instructions. Over a hundred councillors and other worthies appended their signatures, but the Letters never passed the seal, and the original no longer survives. [9] If the copy which does survive is authentic, the intention and method are clear, but the instrument never achieved enforceable status.

Edward died on the 6th July. Mary, warned of what was impending, took herself off to her estates in Norfolk, and mobilised her affinity. The Imperial ambassadors, mindful of their instructions, sat on their hands and waited on events; while the French ambassador, equally mindful of Mary's Imperial connections, offered his king's aid to Northumberland. This time, Mary showed no hesitation. Her legal right was clear, and her support was widespread. On the 8th July she proclaimed herself queen, and called upon her loving subjects for support. At first, Northumberland's momentum carried the council with him. He might, of course, have abandoned his late master's preposterous scheme as soon as the latter was dead, but loyalty or self interest drove him on. Jane was proclaimed in London and at first everyone, including the Imperial ambassadors, thought that the Duke would win. His lead was followed by many local authorities, even in East Anglia, but his position was far less strong than it looked. Most of the council were following him with reluctance, and he had few reliable resources of his own. Mary's proclamations were accepted, and support began to rally to her. Even the protestants, upon whom the Duke had been counting, mostly accepted the lawful heir. By the 19th July Mary had a substantial force at her back, and Northumberland set out to confront her. Almost simultaneously the council divided, London proclaimed Mary, and Jane's cause was lost. There had been no time for French aid to arrive, and Northumberland's apparently impregnable position had collapsed within days.

These dramatic events made an enormous impact, particularly among those who did not understand the dynamics of English politics. [10] Mary was her father's daughter, and Henry had decreed, through parliament, that she should succeed if his son died without heirs. That was sufficient for most people, even protestants. The princess was widely popular, her conservative religious sympathies were at least no handicap, and Northumberland was generally disliked and distrusted. Ironically, this was mainly for nothing worse than having been a successful, if heavy handed, governor for the last three years. The Imperial ambassadors compensated for their inaction by proclaiming a Holy miracle to the whole of Europe, and unfortunately for her, Mary was swept along by the same pious euphoria. In fact the new queen's victory had been brought about by a combination of her own determination, the good organisation of her friends and the unpopularity of her opponents. Mary, however, uneasily aware that she had failed to play the martyr at least twice when opportunities had arisen, now convinced herself that God had preserved her and brought her to the throne, for the specific purposes of restoring true worship and righting the wrongs of the last twenty years. Within a few weeks, or perhaps even days of her accession, she had decided that she must marry swiftly for the sake of the succession (she was already thirty seven), and that she would return the English church to the papal obedience.

Her first task, however, was to form a government, and here she faced considerable difficulties. Because of her strained relations with her brother's council, and her refusal to participate in the high politics of the previous reign, her personal council, although impeccably loyal, lacked any men of political experience. She trusted such men as Sir Robert Rochester and Sir Edward Waldegrave completely, and with good reason. They shared her religious views, and had stood by her with great courage during the dangerous years. However, they had never held positions of greater responsibility than household officers and local justices. Nor were the noblemen who first rallied to her, such as the Earl of Bath, much better from that point of view. Unsurprisingly, they were men who had been at odds with the previous government and excluded from power. Nevertheless, Mary had no option but to form a council as soon as she proclaimed herself queen, and consequently her first, or 'Framlingham' council, so called from the place where it was formed, consisted entirely of such inexperienced enthusiasts. This situation was transformed by the defection of most of the London council to her cause on the 19th July. Lord Paget and the Earl of Arundel, who had the least connection with Northumberland and who had led the defection, immediately hastened into Norfolk to make their submission. They were graciously received, and were followed more slowly by other who were less certain of their welcome. In this tricky situation, Mary acted sensibly. She could not govern the country without the assistance of at least some of these seasoned councillors who were now professing their undying devotion, so she applied her knowledge and common sense to the making of distinctions. Some she welcomed and employed immediately, others, like the Lord Treasurer the Marquis of Winchester, she received coolly and kept waiting for some time before agreeing to accept their services. Others she refused to receive, and consigned to prison. By the time that she reached London on the third of August, she had the makings of a working council, but she was too generous to dispense with her household councillors. As a result the whole body was already rather large (over thirty), and contained a natural fault line between the experienced, who regarded the inexperienced as an encumberance, and the latter, who regarded the former as timeservers of doubtful loyalty. As if this was not sufficiently difficult, Mary then added to the complexities by releasing from confinement those whom she considered to have been wrongfully imprisoned, and welcoming three of them also onto the council, Stephen Gardiner, former bishop of Winchester, Cuthbert Tunstall of Durham, and the Duke of Norfolk. Gardiner she immediately appointed Lord Chancellor. This was one of her best appointments, but set up another tension within the council, because he was at daggers drawn with Lord Paget. Tunstall and Norfolk were both old men whose restoration signified little beyond the victory of sentiment over practical politics.

Mary's government was effectively complete by the end of August. It was probably as good a team as she could have assembled in the circumstances, but contained a number of dangerous weaknesses, not least in its relations with the queen herself. The problem was that the men whom Mary trusted lacked the ability to govern, and those who had the ability she did not fully trust. Inevitably all this latter group had served either her father, or her brother, or both, in the execution of policies which deeply offended her conscience, and she was unable to put that circumstance behind her. She had acted sensibly, but her attitude was less pragmatic. It was partly for this reason that she made an understandable, but serious mistake. As soon as her victory had been assured, the Imperial ambassadors, in addition to issuing their miraculous manifesto, also hastened to ingratiate themselves with the new queen. The leader in this, and soon the sole practitioner, was Simon Renard, an experienced but egotistical diplomat high in the favour of the Bishop of Arras, Charles V's chief minister, who was mainly responsible for dealing with the English situation. [11] Renard quickly established a confidential relationship with Mary, taking advantage of the fact that she had for years regarded Charles as an *alter pater*, and now professed to trust his judgement and advice above all others. This was extremely unwise. The Emperor had not the slighest right to dictate policy to an independent kingdom, and Mary had no right to abdicate her responsibility. On the other hand, the queen was entitled to take her counsel wherever she pleased, and although Renard's position was much resented, it did not much affect the loyalty or the diligence of her own servants.

What it did do was to add another element of division to an already divided council. Some thought that Renard's influence should be resisted as far as possible, others that it was better to go along with it, and milk the Emperor's goodwill for all it was worth. Mary became confused and distressed. Because of her lack of experience of affairs, she appears to have believed that it was the duty of her council to give her unanimous, or at least consensual, advice. However, the whole set up of the council had rendered that virtually impossible, and in any case a councillor's oath only bound him as an individual to advice his sovereign in accordance with his own conscience and understanding. It said nothing about collective advice, or responsibility. A cannier politician, such as Elizabeth, welcomed conflicting advice because it put no pressure upon her to decide one way or another, but Mary, aware of her own limitations, was genuinely seeking guidance. Paradoxically, both the important decisions which she made in the autumn of 1553 would have defied the majority of her council, if she had asked them; but she did not.

### III
### Marriage, plots and policies

Having established her government, Mary had two priorities; to define her legal position and to seek a suitable marriage. The former need was created by her gender. As we have seen, England had never had a ruling Queen, and common lawyers were already expressing the view that she had only a 'woman's estate', that is that the realm would pass to her husband in full ownership on marriage. Consequently it was necessary to resolve that issue before any marriage took place, and thanks to the recently augmented authority of parliament, statute offered a suitable way to do that. The most urgent need, therefore, was to seek a suitable partner. There was not a great deal of choice. Candidates needed to be of royal blood and irreproachable catholicism. Ideally they should also have political and sexual experience, and sufficient resources of their own to outface any opposition which might arise. Mary quickly made it clear to anyone who was willing to listen, that she had no intention of marrying one of her own subjects, and given what happened to Mary Stewart ten years later, that was a sensible decision. Because she was friendly with Gertrude, Marchioness of Exeter, and because she did not take her council into her confidence, the illusion persisted for some time that she would wed Edward Courtenay, Gertrude's son, recently freed from the Tower and created Earl of Devon. [12] Courtenay had influential supporters, notably the Lord Chancellor, but it is clear that Mary never seriously considered him. Among foreign royal families there were just three realistic possibilities. The first was Dom Luis of Portugal, younger brother of the king; the second Maximilian, the son of the Emperor's brother, Ferdinand; and the third was

Charles's own son Philip, Prince of Spain. Dom Luis had sued for her hand before, and with the benefit of hindsight would probably have been the best choice; but Mary put her destiny in the hands of the Emperor and his agent, Simon Renard, and Charles decided that she should marry Philip.

This decision was taken in his own interests, not those of England, but that was Mary's fault, not his. Charles was in poor health, exhausted by his long struggle with France, the Turks and the Lutherans, and intending to abdicate. He had failed to intrude Philip into the Imperial succession, which had been settled on Ferdinand in 1530, and he had distorted the Imperial constitution in order to attach two key territories, Milan and the Low Countries, to Philip's patrimony. In the near future, therefore, he would be handing over the Low Countries to Philip, who was not popular there. This transition was likely to be challenged, not only by the French but also by his Austrian cousins, with whom his relations at this juncture were poor. The opportunity to marry Philip to Mary was therefore extremely welcome, because it would give Philip a power base in northern Europe from which to secure his position in the Low Countries. Charles knew enough about the queen's medical history to be deeply sceptical of her ability to produce a healthy child. Of course, if there were a son of the union, the prospect of establishing a further Habsburg power bloc in the north, and completing the encirclement of France, was exhilarating. But it was also a remote possibility, and the Emperor was not counting upon it. None of these thoughts did he share with his son, who was excluded from the negotiations. However, when Mary's servants set out to redeem their mistress's rash commitment by extracting a favourable treaty from Charles, they found him surprisingly complaisant. He was happy to settle the Low Countries, along with England, on any child of the union, detatching them from Spain. He agreed that Philip should have no power in England except in conjunction with Mary, that he should use only English servants when in the country, and that he should undertake not to drag England into his perennial conflict with France. A treaty on these lines was concluded in January 1554, and immediately proclaimed.

The reason for this was that opposition to the match had been building, and the actual treaty was far more generous than had been reported. England was not to become just another Habsburg matrimonial conquest. The deal was not a bad one in the circumstances. Philip was a widower of twenty six, with one son, and had governed Spain in his father's name for several years. He was also a zealous catholic. It was a very good idea to keep on good terms with the master of the Low Countries, whether present or future, because it was the destination of so much English trade, and to be locked into a firm alliance with one of Europe's two superpowers. It was even possible to concoct a distant connection with the Plantagenet royal family, and to claim that the Prince had English origins! [13] On the other hand, when Philip became ruler of Spain, with its enormous empire and world-wide commitments, he would not only have little time to intervene in English affairs, he was likely to become a permanent absentee. Opponents of the union, who had at first included several councillors and the House of Commons, argued that Philip would inevitably seek to impose himself and his own agenda, and that he had the power to override all objections. England would become a Spanish dependency, and face endless wars in the Habsburg interest. Once it had become clear that Mary had made her decision, her councillors all accepted it with a reasonably good grace, and opposition became concentrated in a small section of the aristocracy, who feared displacement by the king's Spanish servants.

Many doubts surround this group. Some of them were former supporters of Jane Grey, and some were apprehensive protestants, but most seem to have been religious conformists, who had supported Mary in the previous summer. They were egged on by the French ambassador, Antoine de Noailles, who was desperate to sabotage a marriage so contrary to French interests. They professed loyalty to the queen, and a desire merely to persuade her to change her mind and marry within the realm. However, it seems clear that their real intention was to dispossess Mary in favour of her half sister Elizabeth. A disgruntled Edward Courtenay was marginally involved, and it was through him that the conspiracy came to light. Faced with his inconvenient disclosures, the conspiritors were forced to act long before they were ready, or French aid could be provided. Attempts to raise the South West and the Midlands failed, and the rebellion is usually known by the name of its only successful leader, Sir Thomas Wyatt. In January 1554 Wyatt raised a force of about 3000 men in Kent, and menaced London. In itself his power was not great, but he overwhelmed the first two attempts to resist him in the Queen's name, and there was panic at court. Encouraged by Renard, Mary showed coolness and resolution. She went to Guildhall and appealed for the loyalty of the citizens of London. Several powerful noblemen belatedly rallied to her, and the crisis passed. Although it lasted only a few days, it had been a dangerous episode, and left a number of traces behind. About 400 were executed and the opposition was suppressed; but it was not appeased in spite of the treaty, and Renard continued to be nervous. He persuaded the council to arrest Elizabeth and Courtenay, and consign them to the Tower, but he could not persuade the Queen to execute either of them. Unless or until the queen's marriage bore fruit, Elizabeth was her heir in law and Renard believed, probably correctly, that she was a serious rival for English loyalties. Equally important, he remained convinced that there was disaffection within the Queen's government, for which he principally blamed the Chancellor, Stephen Gardiner. This was mistaken, and spread unnecessary confusion, but he was right to suspect the Queen's popularity, so high the previous summer, was already waning.

He was also undermined by Philip. The Prince had been outraged when he discovered the terms of the treaty which his father had negotiated for him. His servants and courtiers were even more horrified by the powerless and dishonourable position which awaited him in England. He considered repudiating the whole agreement, but eventually confined himself to a solemn declaration that he did not intend to observe the terms of the treaty - which was precisely what his enemies in England were suggesting he would do. [14] Meanwhile, he took his dissatisfaction out on Renard, deliberately keeping him in the dark about his intentions. Philip's displeasure was also manifested in a general lack of communication. He neither wrote nor sent any token to his bride, and even the betrothal *per verba de praesenti* in March passed without comment from him. He was having genuine difficulties in arranging for the government of Spain in what was bound to be a prolonged absence, and that explains his delay, but not his silence. It was July before he eventually reached England, bringing with him a full Spanish household; either genuinely or ostensibly ignorant of the fact that an English household awaited him, and that he had bound himself to use English servants while in England. In the circumstance it is quite surprising that his first encounter with his bride was affectionate almost to point of tenderness, and that they were married in Winchester cathedral on the 25th July with great splendour and not a sign of hostile demonstration. The French had not attempted to intervene, and Renard felt inclined to celebrate another miracle. However, there were rocks below the smooth surface. The double household caused endless trouble, in spite of the king's diplomacy; hostility between two proud and tetchy people was constantly surfacing; and Mary was even less attractive physically than Philip had feared. He grumbled discreetly to trusted fellow countrymen, while remaining scrupulously polite and attentive in public to the woman who he continued to refer to in private as *tia mia* - my aunt.

Philip's safe arrival solved a number of problems. It enhanced the queen's security by discrediting the forces of opposition, which had threatened much, and achieved nothing. It removed Renard from his confidential and anomalous position, and it opened the way for an answer to the question of what to do about the church. Parliament had ratified the marriage treaty in April, and at the same time had removed disquiet about the 'woman's estate' by declaring that the queen's authority was the same as that of any of her predecessors 'kings of this realm'. In other words that gender disability did not apply to the Crown. [15] Mary had earlier taken the precaution of having herself declared legitimate and lawful queen by statute, and these two acts together represented almost as great an enhancement of the jurisdiction of parliament as the Act of Supremacy itself. As we have seen, the queen had early disclosed her intention of returning the church to Rome. This took all except her intimates by surprise, as her declared position over the previous fifteen years had been to support her father's settlement. Whether, or how many times, she had changed her mind is not clear. On the Emperor's instructions, Renard discouraged her. They both believed that protestant sentiment was strong, and that whereas opposition to a Henrician reaction was likely to be muted, the pope would be a red rag to a bull. This was exaggerated, but not wildly so. In fact the restoration of traditional worship, particularly the mass, was generally welcomed, although there were some hostile demonstrations in London, and was accomplished by statute in the second session of her first parliament. On the 20th December 1553 the protestant prayer book went out of use, and at about the same time campaigns against married clergy and 'intruded' bishops began. Mary had simply ignored the Edwardian deprivations of conservative bishops, on the inaccurate assumption that they had been unlawful, and treated protestantism in general as though it had been merely a confidence trick worked by ambitious politicians. She took the circumstances of her accession as a general endorsement of her religious position, and was unreasonably disconcerted when parliament at first refused to resurrect the see of Durham, and her nobles made it clear that they would not accept the papal jurisdiction without a guarantee for their former monastic property. To Mary religious truth was so self evident that she could not conceive of any honest dissent. Her ministers, however, did not share her naivety. Stephen Gardiner realised perfectly well that the Emperor's caution was in a sense artificial. He did not want to stir up unnecessary opposition, but he also wanted his son to get the credit for a high profile reconciliation. The Chancellor, however, also realised that it would be a poor strategy to bring back the pope in the train of a foreign king. He tried to persuade parliament to annul the royal supremacy in April 1554, before Philip's arrival, but was frustrated by Paget, perhaps acting out of genuinely patriotic concern, but more likely with one eye on the Imperial interest. Rather surprisingly, Mary understood Gardiner's purpose, and supported it. She was consequently furious with Paget, who was lucky to avoid imprisonment, and greeted the king whose cause he had done so much to promote, in deep disgrace.

Mary stopped using the obnoxious title of Supreme Head in December 1553, but she continued to use the authority which went with it in order to enforce the return of the Henrician compromise. Protestant preachers were arrested and imprisoned, and Gardiner did his best (not very succ-essfully) to chivvy those continental protestants who had taken refuge in England in the previous reign back to their places of origin. [16] There was, as yet, no persecution, because there was, in Mary's eyes, no proper ecclesiastical jurisdiction to conduct it. However, with Philip's safe arrival the Emperor's caution disappeared, and he threw his weight behind a campaign for the swift ending of the English schism.

## IV
## The catholic restoration, and persecution

In spite of the queen's expressed intention, and the efforts of Stephen Gardiner, the church which welcomed Philip in July 1554 was still the schismatic church which Henry VIII had left. Mary had assuaged her troubled conscience by importing special chrisom from the Low Countries for her coronation, but she was both crowned and married by schismatic bishops. She had used every resource of her authority to restore conservative bishops, deprive protestants, and make satisfactory new appointments, but none of them were catholics in the full and proper sense. Pope Julius III was well aware of this, and was becoming increasingly frustrated. He had appointed the only English born Cardinal, Reginald Pole, as legate to negotiate the reconciliation as soon as the news of Mary's accession had reached him. Since then Pole had been in regular touch with the queen, and with some other English catholics, but his mission had made no progress. This was partly because of the Emperor's attitude, as we have seen, and the influence which he had over Mary, but it was also partly because of the cardinal's own views. Pole had known the queen since she was a small child, and had even been mentioned as a possible husband. He was of the royal Plantagenet blood, and Mary had great respect for his learning and piety. [17] However, he had written to her immediately after his appointment, urging her to declare her allegiance to the Holy See at once, on the grounds that all the statutes which had enforced the Royal Supremacy were *ipso facto* invalid and null. This was a logical view, and privately Mary probably agreed with him, but in the context of English politics it was unrealistic and self defeating. In theory the Royal Supremacy had not been created by statute, but merely recognised, and the only lawful way to annul an Act of Parliament was to repeal it. Mary accepted the advice of her council, that the only safe way to undo the religious settlements of her father and brother was through parliament. Little as she, or Pole, may have liked the idea, from now on the Catholic church in England would have to be the Church by law established.

The English council felt, rightly, that Pole would have had a seriously disruptive effect upon the delicate political situation in Mary's first year, and the queen made no protest when Charles halted the Legate's progress towards England. By the summer of 1554 much had been achieved. Edward's settlement had gone and the protests, although vociferous had been small scale. Gardiner had partly succeeded in discrediting the protestants by blaming them for Wyatt's rebellion; many leading protestants, including the Duke of Northumberland, had apostasised; and a number of the most active leaders had gone into exile. Once Philip was established, it was time to move on to the next phase, because the king had, what Mary did not, enormous influence in Rome. In spite of the handicap of speaking no English, Philip soon realised that the big obstacle to repealing the Henrician acts was the attitude of those whom Pole called 'the possessioners'; that is those who had purchased from the crown property which had formerly belonged to the church. They knew perfectly well that the papacy had never accepted Henry's right to appropriate that property, and would therefore deny that they had any legal title to it. This obstacle had to be overcome, and the only way to do that was to persuade Julius to renounce the church's rights in return for a formal submission. Mary could never have achieved that, but Philip, with his father's backing, had the necessary weight. After intense negotiation in the autumn of 1554, Julius gave way; Pole's long standing attainder was reversed, and he was invited to return to England and carry out his mission.

The cardinal made a conciliatory speech to the Lords and Commons, and parliament petitioned the King and Queen to sue for absolution in the name of the whole realm. The battle, however, was not yet over. Pole made it clear that in his view the 'possessioners' were entitled to retain their property simply because the dispensation which he was authorised to issue absolved them from the sin of unlawful expropriation. There was, and could be, no transfer of legal title. This was not good enough for the English lawyers. A dispensation which one pope had issued, another could withdraw; as a safeguard of rights, it was useless. Something better than that would be needed before the Henrician statutes were repealed, and an ingenious scheme was worked out. By including the full text of the papal dispensation in the statute of repeal, it could be given the force of English law, and would therefore remain binding no matter what any future pope might say, unless or until some future parliament rescinded it. This made no sense to Pole, and he resisted the

12

proposal, with Mary's support. Both Philip and the Privy Council, however, could see the lawyers' point, and supported the idea. Philip must have talked the queen round, because she did not persist in her opposition, and Pole could do nothing without her support. Mary's second Repeal Act became law at the end of the parliamentary session on 16 January 1555. The Royal Supremacy came to an end; papal jurisdiction was restored; and the owners of monastic property had a title which they could plead in the English courts. [18] Pole was now authorised to exercise his Legatine powers, and immediately began to issue commissions for the investigation and trial of heresy.

This was the high water mark of Mary's reign. So far, her husband had been everything that she hoped he would be, and since October she had been convinced that she was carrying his child. She had successfully defeated all opposition, and restored the church to the unity of Christendom. For the protestants, on the other hand, the time of trial had now come. Neither Mary nor Gardiner took their professions seriously. The queen simply could not comprehend how anyone could fail to accept the truth of the faith which she embraced, and believed that they were either play acting or inspired by the Devil. Gardiner, slightly more practical, saw them as ambitious men playing for high stakes. They had been ousted from power, and were plotting to return by any means possible. A show of resolution and integrity might win them support, and enable another and more formidable Wyatt rebellion to be raised, which this time the French would not fail to support. To Mary, and to Pole, the punishment of heretics was a sacred duty, to protect the main body of the faithful from a deadly contamination which would ruin them body and soul. To Gardiner it was a policy designed to defeat a crafty and potentially dangerous enemy. Both sides watched the first trials in January 1555 with acute anxiety. The policy was to go first for high profile leaders, not necessarily the highest in rank, but the most popular and respected. Within a few days John Hooper, the former bishop of Worcester and Gloucester, Rowland Taylor, the Rector of Hadleigh, John Cardmaker, John Rogers, John Bradford and Lawrence Saunders were arraigned and condemned. Gardiner hoped and believed that they would submit, thus discrediting their whole position in the eyes of their followers. In the event only Cardmaker did so; the remainder stood firm, and were burned at the stake. Inspired by this example, a steady stream of similar victims then followed. Renard, still in England but virtually without influence, wrote to the Emperor in alarm, saying that the bishops' severity must be checked before it provoked rebellion. Philip, who was not squeamish about persecution, but realised that as an unpopular foreigner he was likely to get the blame, discreetly distanced himself from what was going on, and even encouraged one of his chaplains to preach against it.

In April 1555 the three highest ranking protestants still in custody, Cranmer, Ridley and Latimer, were taken to Oxford to confront the academic champions of both universities. The intention of this move was not to discredit their courage or pertinacity, but their learning. Their theology was to be revealed as inconsistent, unsoundly based, and a product of mere intellectual arrogance. Latimer, once bishop of Worcester and a famous preacher, was by this time an old man, and refused to play the role allotted to him. He reaffirmed his faith in relatively simple terms, but refused to be drawn into formal disputation. Nicholas Ridley, the Edwardian bishop of London, was an altogether tougher proposition. Disconcerted by the vigour and coherence of his responses, his opponents tried to anger and unnerve him by discarding the formal rules on which they were supposed to be operating, and inviting 'audience participation'. Ridley was certainly angered, but not much deflected, and certainly not prepared to yield an inch. Thomas Cranmer was, by virtue of the fact that he had been papally confirmed in 1533, still Archbishop of Canterbury. He was also, however, a 'dead man' in law because he had been condemned for high treason as a Privy Councillor who had supported the Duke of Northumberland's plot. He had not been executed because Mary believed his heresy to be a more serious offence than his treason, and also because she did not want to execute an Archbishop until he had been formally degraded. Cranmer was attacked upon a range of issues which were ecclesiatical rather than theological. He had married (twice); he had broken his oath of loyalty to the Pope; and having proclaimed his loyalty to the Crown and to the law of the land, he was now defying both by refusing to return to the old faith. By comparison with Ridley, Cranmer's performance was unimpressive. He could not deny the charges, and it is not surprising that his opponents found his rejoinders feeble. On strictly theological issues he was learned and inflexible, but on other matters he gave the impression of a man unsure of his ground. Unsurprisingly, what was virtually a show trial ended with the protestants being declared defeated, and exposed as undoubted heretics. It was not a judicial tribunal, and they could not be condemned or punished as a result, so it is difficult to see what the authorities gained by the exercise. In spite of a triumphalist declaration at the end, no attempt was made to publish or otherwise capitalise upon the disputations, so as an exercise in public humiliation its impact was confined to those who had actually been present. The surviving accounts of what transpired all come from the protestant side.

By the summer of 1555 the persecution was settling into a lethal routine. In the dioceses of London, Canterbury, Rochester and Norwich a steady procession of protestants was passing through the processes of inquisition. Some submitted, a few escaped, but the majority were imprisoned and many were burned. These were both men and women, young and old, and most were humble people. There were a handful of clergy and an even smaller number of yeomen and gentlemen, but the majority were artisans or husbandmen, and many of the women were servants. Outside these areas the number was smaller, widely and erratically spread. Parts of the north and west were not touched at all. Where burnings took place, the public reaction was usually hostile. We do not need to take the elaborate narratives of Foxe's *Acts and Monuments* too literally to accept that these people frequently suffered an appalling death with great courage. They were usually, and deliberately burned in their own communities as a terrible example to others, but their attitude often caused the example to backfire. There was little of the spirit of the *auto da fe* in England, and independent testimony such as that of the Venetian ambassador suggests that the government gained little credit by its severity. Long before he died in November 1555 Stephen Gardiner had concluded that as a policy, the persecution had failed, and that the government would be well advised to use lower profile methods of dealing with what had become an unexpectedly intransigent problem.

Neither Mary nor Pole heeded this advice, and the persecution ground on, counting almost 300 victims before the queen's death brought it to an abrupt conclusion. This was severe, even by contemporary European standards, and left an indelible impression. [19] In many respects the catholic restoration went well. The damaged jurisdiction and depleted resources of the church recovered under Pole's energetic administration, particularly after Cranmer's degredation and execution in March 1556 also elevated him to the see of Canterbury. The restoration of traditional rites and usages was generally welcomed, and most of the clergy who had married under the previous regime renounced their wives and were transferred to other benefices. Some of the queen's council, and some local justices, became enthusiastic persecutors. Nevertheless, the protestants gained enormously in credibility once they were no longer the beneficiaries of a sympathetic regime. The word 'martyr' began to be used, and not only by protestant polemicists. Also, in spite of the publication of a fine set of *Homilies* by Edmund Bonner, the bishop of London, and a number of other works of catholic piety, the process of 'reconversion' was fitful and lacking in zeal. Mary seems to have believed that no such process was needed, although she supported 'good' preaching. Pole took the opposite view, believing that preaching was disruptive, but that the quality of faith needed to be enhanced by devotional instruction. Above all, he wanted to improve clerical education, and made that a prime objective in the Legatine Synod which he convened in 1556.

However, before that meeting could even run its course, the Cardinal's world had fallen apart. His friend Julius III had died in March 1555, and been succeeded by the elderly Neapolitan Carafa as Paul IV. Pole and Carafa had been on opposite sides during the doctrinal debates of the 1540s, and the latter was convinced that the Englishman was a heretic. At first he confirmed Pole's status in England, and appeared to endorse his policies; but in the spring of 1557 he cancelled his mission and recalled him to face trial in Rome. Philip and Mary refused to allow their archbishop to obey the summons, and the newly restored relationship between Rome and the English church was consigned to the refrigerator. Pole was devastated, and did little more than go through the motions during the last year of his life. Meanwhile the English protestants in exile were conducting an increasingly radical and effective campaign against Mary, linking her Spanish and Roman sympathies (quite unjustifiably) to the unprecedented holocaust of the persecution. By November 1558 time was not necessarily on the Queen's side.

## V
## Philip as King

In spite of the unexpected cordiality with which he had been greeted, and the successful start of his relationship with Mary, Philip was not a happy man. His Spanish courtiers, and more particularly their wives, treated the English with contempt, and were repaid with bitter hostility. He soon got rid of most of them, but a core problem remained. Because he spoke no English, and his French was poor, he was reluctant to allow any but Spaniards into his personal service. At the same time, his position as king required that he be served in public by his English officers. As a result the English complained that they were allowed no access to the Privy Chamber, and the Spaniards complained that they were dishonoured by being kept in the background. Philip did his best to placate this feud, but it dogged him throughout his stay. Quarrels were frequent, and violence occasional. Both sides were guilty, and the king's attempts at evenhandedness were misrepresented by both sides. Mary was distressed, but found no way to solve the problem herself. With the council, and with senior ecclesiastics like Gardiner, there were fewer problems because he had a good command of Latin, and interpreters were available.

Philip's first, and most important involvement in the public affairs of England was in the negotiations for reconciliation with Rome. This was a role in which his father had caste him, and he was willing enough. During the autumn and winter of 1554 Habsburg propaganda celebrated in several languages the triumph of the Prince of Spain in England. [20] Charles had created him King of Naples just before his nuptials, so that he could marry Mary as an equal, but had made no attempt to hand over the government of that kingdom to him. However the success of the English negotiation raised Philip's prestige higher than his father's, and began the conversion of the Imperial party in the papal curia into the Spanish party which it was to be after 1560. Meanwhile the Franco-Imperial war which had been going on since 1551 became stalemated, leaving Philip freer to attend to English business. Had Mary only known it, she had narrowly avoided being abandoned almost on the steps of the church. Alarmed by French advances in June 1554, the Emperor had instructed his son to spend only a few days in England after his marriage, before proceeding to the battlefront in the Netherlands. Fortunately the advance was turned back, the order countermanded in the nick of time, and Philip stayed with his bride. Hardly anyone knew of this crisis at the time, which was just as well because it would have confirmed the doubts which many English sceptics still retained, as to where Habsburg priorities really lay.

The king's position was difficult, and he was forced to call upon reserves of self discipline which many (including his father) did not believe him to possess. For reasons which remain obscure, Mary gave him no English patrimony. It was customary in England for a consort to be granted a life interest in an extensive estate, providing an income similar to that of a major peer; but Philip received nothing. He consequently had to pay and reward his English servants out of his Spanish revenues. He also had no English residence of his own. The parliament did somewhat reluctantly extend the protection of the treason laws to him, and granted him the governorship of any child who might be born to the queen, should she predecease him, leaving an heir under age. His Spanish servants grumbled loudly (and justifiably) about his lack of authority, but consoled themselves with the thought that when Mary's child was born, the whole situation would change. Although as Mary's supposed pregnancy advanced she became less active, Philip did not thrust himself forward. He appears to have had regular consultations with the council, and the Queen listened to his advice with respect, but circumstances conspired to keep most of his attention focussed on events in Europe. In spite of efforts which were made to 'sell' him to the English - particularly the pageantry surrounding his entry into London - he achieved little popularity. [21] His relations with the English aristocracy, on the other hand, made good progress. Many of them were his pensioners, and those who found it hard to accept that their sovereign was a woman looked to him for 'real' leadership, particularly military employment. By the spring of 1555 he had the makings of a useful party among the English peers.

However, the failure of Mary's pregnancy in July 1555 changed the whole situation. This bizarre sequence of events left the queen emotionally and physically exhausted, and forced Philip to reassess his position. There was now little chance that Mary, who was thirty nine, would ever have a healthy child. England, therefore, was only likely to be available to him as long as she lived; and the hoped for enhancement of his authority would not now happen unless he took some steps himself to loosen the restraints of the marriage treaty. At the same time, he was urgently needed in the Netherlands, and had remained in England so long only to 'cover' the queen's confinement. He made practical arrangements to keep in touch with the English council through a somewhat notional body called the 'council of state', and in August, while Mary was still convalescent, departed to the continent. There he immediately became preoccupied with the process of taking over authority from his father, and negotiating a cessation of hostilities with the French. A few members of his English household accompanied him during the first weeks, but since he had been barred from using his own servants in public affairs in England, he had no inclination to employ Englishmen elsewhere, and they soon returned home. Over the next eighteen months his influence fluctuated somewhat unpredictably. He was persuaded, possibly by unsound legal advice, that he should make a major effort to secure coronation in England. If this had immediately followed his wedding, it would probably have passed without comment, but seeking it as and when he did inevitably aroused suspicion. He must have been trying to recover the credibility which he had lost by the failure of Mary's pregnancy, but whether he was really trying to circumvent the marriage treaty remains uncertain. His efforts were soon noticed by his critics in England, and denounced in extravagant terms. When Mary urged him to return and take a hand in English affairs, he replied in effect that he would do so only on his own terms, and those terms included a coronation. The queen's reaction is puzzling. She wanted Philip back, both for personal and political reasons; she missed him both as a councillor and as a husband; and whatever anyone else might think, she had not given up hope of issue. On the other hand, she was quite unwilling to meet his terms. Having virtually ignored parliament in her determination to marry him, she now pleaded parliamentary opposition in refusing a coronation. He pointed out, quite rightly, that it was none of parliament's business, but she was not to be persuaded. When Gardiner the Lord Chancellor and the earl of Bedford, the Lord Privy Seal died during 1555, Philip played an important part in the choice of

Nicholas Heath and Lord Paget to replace them; but his contact with the English council seems to have waned after the end of 1555.

What brought Mary and Philip back together for a while was not solicitude on his part, or surrender on hers, but war. Almost as soon as Charles had handed over the crowns of Spain to his son in January 1556, the truce of Vaucelles suspended the Franco-Habsburg conflict. Ironically, this did not suit the pope. Paul IV, as a Neapolitan, nursed a bitter hatred of the Habsburgs and all their works, which he could gratify by supporting the French while the war persisted. Consequently when hostilities ceased, he devoted his diplomatic energies to getting them started again. For months he deliberately provoked Philip, confident that the French would come to his aid if (or when) the Spaniards attacked.

The Duke of Alba finally obliged on the 1st September 1556 by invading the papal states. For a few months hostilities were confined to Italy, but in February 1557 the French finally broke the truce in the north, and full scale war recommenced. Philip's resources were seriously overstretched, and he needed England's assistance; moreover, he was king of England, and it would be detrimental to his honour if any of his realms hung back. The English council thought otherwise, arguing not only that the realm was poor and could not afford war, but that this was the same war that was covered by the marriage treaty, having been interrupted only by a truce. Councils, however, did not make decisions of war and peace, and Mary on this issue supported her husband. He returned to England in March 1557, without making any preconditions, and aided by a timely descent of English exiles on the Yorkshire coast (plausibly, but probably wrongly, blamed on French initiative), succeeded in forcing a declaration of war. [22] England's military aristocracy rallied to the king, and when he returned to the continent in July he was followed by a sizeable English expeditionary force, commanded by the Earl of Pembroke, for which he footed the bill.

Mary never saw him again. The English expeditionary force performed well at first, but was back home by October, and the war effort petered out. In January 1558 the French took Calais, and Philip found himself being blamed. By then he was losing interest in England. Mary was clearly never going to have a child, and he would not be able to extend his control over the realm in the event of her death without a major military effort which he could not afford. His English pensions fell heavily into arrears as their priority declined in his hard up Exchequer, and he no longer bothered to maintain a party among the English nobility. From about 1556 onward he began to shift his attention to what would happen next. Mary's dislike of her half sister Elizabeth was notorious, but she had had no success in finding an alternative heir. Both Mary Stewart and the surviving Grey sisters were ruled out for obvious reasons, and the Queen's own favourite, Margaret Douglas, raised not a flicker of interest. [23] By 1557 Philip had concluded that Elizabeth would succeed, and the best policy would be to marry her to a reliable dependent of the Habsburgs. His candidate was Emmanuel Philibert, Duke of Savoy, who could, if necessary, be spared for the difficult job of being King of England, and might stand a better chance of being accepted than Philip himself. Unsurprisingly Elizabeth, who was determined to keep her options open, refused all advances. Philip could not compel her, and Mary, who could have done, was unwilling. As with her failure to give her husband a patrimony, or a coronation, the queen's refusal to coerce her sister into a marriage which Philip so much desired - and for such good reason - is an unsolved mystery. Consequently as Mary's health deteriorated in the summer of 1558, Philip found himself dealing as an equal with a very tough minded young woman, who was aware that time was on her side and was determined to give nothing away. That the king fell in love with his young sister in law is a romantic embellishment, but he certainly came to respect her political talents.

As Mary's life was visibly drawing to close in October 1558, Philip's main reaction seems to have been one of relief. He urgently needed a fruitful consort who would give him more children,

17

and if the queen had lived much longer he might have had to seek an annulment, and that would have been a personal tragedy which Mary did not deserve. In fact he had gained a good deal from the marriage, in spite of all the difficulties. His position in the Low Countries was not challenged, and the prestige which he gained in Rome from negotiating the end of the English schism long outlasted the achievement itself. In England, he achieved little, and was remembered without affection. It has been claimed that he revitalised the English navy, and he was certainly keenly interested in it, as being the only military asset in which England was pre-eminent, but his supposed intervention does not stand close scrutiny.[24] He also fell out bitterly with the merchant community of London, consistently supporting their Flemish and Hanseatic rivals, and doing his best to prevent them from expanding their enterprise into West Africa. Those who had supported the marriage on the grounds that it would bring English access to the closed world of Spanish American trade, were totally disappointed. In 1553 it had seemed a sensible policy to cement the traditional 'Burgundian alliance' in this way, and secure long term protection against French aggression, but by 1558 even its keenest advocates, such as Lord Paget, were disillusioned with the result. Henry VIII had defied the world, and that was one reason why his subjects remembered his capricious and often tryannical regime with nostalgia. His elder daughter showed no such independence of spirit, and her attitude towards her husband was a strange mixture of wifely subservience and wilful defiance.

Perhaps it was really Charles rather than Philip that Mary wanted to obey, and the king was only too willing to set his English adventure behind him. Over the next thirty years he was to become a bogeyman to frighten English children in their cradles.


# VI
## Dynastic failure and opposition

The failure of Mary's pregnancy was the turning point of her reign. Up to that point she had enjoyed a remarkable degree of success. In spite of mistakes resulting from inexperience, and the priority which she conceded to her inflexible conscience, she had achieved most of her objectives. Even in the matter of public finance, in which she had no expertise at all, the situation was improving. During the last year of Edward's reign strict control by the Duke of Northumberland, and sensible advice from London financiers such as Thomas Gresham had reduced the Crown debt from about £250,000 to about £180,000, and stabilised the exchange rate of sterling in Antwerp. Mary, as usual, gave the first priority to her conscience. She wrote off the outstanding instalment of the subsidy voted by Edward's last parliament, apparently on the unfounded assumption that it had been an unjust extortion; and she borrowed a large sum in Spain, because that was what Charles advised her to do. Both these were mistakes, and put the debt level back to where it had been in 1552. However, after that she was persuaded to let the Marquis of Winchester get on with his job, and working closely with the London merchants, he began to get the debt level down again. By the summer of 1555 the corner had been turned. As the queen prepared for her confinement, there were obvious worries about her own life. Elizabeth, who had been in various forms of confinement for over a year following the Wyatt rebellion, was brought to court in May 1555. This was not so much release as a different form of restraint, but no attempt had been made to exclude her from the succession. Nothing was said, but it was recognised that if Mary died in childbirth, she would be queen.

The prevailing atmosphere, however, was positive. Although the protestants were proving to be an unexpected nuisance, they were no more than that. God had been good to Mary. He had raised

18

her to the throne against the odds; he had given her a powerful, and apparently loving, husband; he had protected her against rebels and conspiritors; and he had used her to restore his own true worship.

There was, however, a major snag to using tangible success as a measure of divine approval. Where did you stand when the luck changed? The protestants had already been forced to confront that one, and had come up with various embellishments upon 'whom he loveth, he chasteneth'. In other words, worldly success is a mere delusion. The Elect are always being afflicted or persecuted to put their faith to the test. More specifically, the Edwardian regime had failed, not because it was trying to do the wrong things, but because it had done them so badly. The reign of Josias had been a wasted opportunity for true godliness, and as a result the Elect had now been returned to their accustomed role as victims. Some (but not all) thought that this test would also come to an end, and that the Godly would be given another chance in England, but no one put a timetable to that eventuality. Mary had had her own share of misfortune, and never seems to have believed that it was any particular mark of favour, but the circumstance of her accession had confirmed her in the belief that God intended to use her for his own purposes.

However by the end of July the ways of the Lord had become opaque indeed. Instead of the hoped for child, Mary produced nothing. Her whole condition had been a pathological delusion and probably (although that was not understood at the time) the symptom of a serious illness. The bonfires which had been lit on the release of mistaken tidings petered out; the proclamations and letters of announcement remained unused in the archive. It would be difficult to say who was more embarrassed, the physicians who had so confidently predicted a live birth, or the clergy who had praised God for his continuing goodness.

Quite suddenly, the political landscape changed. Philip, as we have seen, departed for the Low Countries as soon as he decently could, and began to reassess his position. The queen remained prostrate, and picked herself up only slowly over the next few months. Then the harvest failed. The summer weather was wet and wretched, and the crop yield (as far as it can be calculated) one of the worst of the century. Hunger and social disruption threatened. In November the Lord Chancellor Stephen Gardiner died, removing the ablest of the Queen's ministers, and a man whose pragmatic common sense would soon be much missed. In his place was appointed the mild mannered Nicholas Heath, Archbishop of York, who was quite incapable of filling such large shoes. The House of Commons in the parliament which assembled on the 21st October was unusually fractious; not because (as the Venetian ambassador thought) it contained an unusually large number of gentlemen, but because the long term prospects of the government had suddenly become clouded. Invited to confiscate the property of those who had fled into exile for religious dissent, the Commons declined. Too much should not be made of this defiance. It was an isolated event, but it was a straw in the wind, and Mary was angry and distressed. She had not suddenly lost her popularity. That had declined significantly from the peak of two years earlier, but not because of her false pregnancy. What she had lost was a large measure of the credibility which her successful years had given her. Those who were beginning to argue that a ruler who persecuted the saints of God could not expect to enjoy his favour were sounding more plausible.

However, the queen recovered and a semblance of normality was restored. There were isolated bread riots, but no major uprisings. Germs of discontent, however, continued to breed; and some of those who had led the resistance to the 'exiles bill' became infected. The resulting conspiracy is normally known by the name of Henry Dudley, a cousin of the Duke of Northumberland who had taken refuge in France. [25] Insofar as it can be pieced together, it looks rather far fetched and optimistic. The original intention was to raise a force of English exiles in France, establish contact with disgruntled gentry in England, and launch an invasion with French backing. This was almost exactly what Henry of Richmond had done successfully in 1485. The conspiritors were very discreet about their real intentions, talking mainly about getting rid of 'foreigners', that is the Spaniards, but their real purpose was almost certainly to depose Mary in favour of Elizabeth. Henry II, however, drew back. He had just signed the truce of Vaucelles, and although he would be prepared to break that in his own good time, that time was not yet. Wiser men might have desisted at that point, but the plot had clearly developed some momentum. Although some of the lesser conspiritors later fell over themselves to accuse each other, the full ramifications of the plot within the English political nation were never uncovered. Taking advantage of contacts among the queen's servants, a scheme was evolved for relieving the Exchequer of some £50,000 in silver bullion. This would have been used to hire the ships and mercenaries which the king of France was no longer willing to provide; and improbable as it may sound, it came within an ace of success. In the event the plotters were betrayed. Those within reach were arrested, interrogated, and several of them executed. Many remained out of reach in France, and investigations into the extent of gentry involvement petered out in a manner which Mary's more ardent admirers considered highly suspicious. Elizabeth, who had learned wisdom after her brush with Wyatt, was untouched by this latest alarm. The real extent of the danger is hard to assess. What is actually known does not look very threatening, especially given the propensity of malcontents to talk big and do little, but the queen and her council were seriously alarmed at the time, and continued to be apprehensive, even after the ostensible ringleaders had been executed.

1556 was a hard year. Philip stayed away, and imposed stringent conditions for his return. The queen remained depressed and lethargic. The council drove the religious persecution forward against the wishes of many of the 'front line' bishops, including Bonner of London. [26] Thomas Cranmer, who had seemed to promise a spectacular recantation, withdrew his submission at the stake, and turned the propaganda victory on its head. Humble victims began to be despatched in batches, without any serious attempts to obtain recantations. The harvest was again poor, and although largescale starvation was avoided, undernourishment contributed to the virulent outbreak of influenza, which was reaching epidemic proportions by the end of the year. In the autumn Philip and the Pope went to war, and Pole's situation in England became extremely delicate. From his point of view it was a blessing that the king stayed away, but he had now no reliable access to the power mechanisms of the curia, and English business became increasingly neglected. However, the news was not all bad. The financial situation continued to improve, with the aid of a subsidy voted, after some dispute, in the autumn of 1555. Under the efficient leadership of Lord Paget, the council was functioning effectively as a working executive, and probably benefited from the Queen's somewhat sporadic devotion to business. A review of the navy was undertaken in January, and a year later, in January 1557 a new system of financial control was introduced which for the first time gave the service a fixed budget and enabled a proper maintenance programme to be developed.

When Mary welcomed her husband back in March 1557, it may well have seemed that the worst was over. The Queen had survived her disappointment, her opponents had again been defeated, and there was no serious resistance to her government anywhere in the realm. When war broke out, not everyone was disappointed. There was a 'war party' in the council which believed that the country would rally more effectively behind the queen in fighting the 'ancient enemy'; and professional soldiers whom Mary had regarded with mistrust now looked for employment in the king's armies. The surviving sons of the Duke of Northumberland, Ambrose, Henry and Robert, who had been released early in 1555, but kept at arms length, were similarly recruited. [27] It looked for a while as though the war would become a healer of the divisions which afflicted England. Moreover Mary, having spent another four months in her husband's company, became convinced again that she was pregnant. On the previous occasion there had been great fanfares of expectation; a nursery had been prepared, wet nurses and rockers appointed; ambassadors briefed. This time there was no warning, but a bald announcement from the queen in January 1558 that she was expecting a child, and had refrained from making any announcement in order to make sure, after her previous experience. In 1555 her condition had been seriously discussed in every court in Europe, but this time the reaction was one of amused incredulity. Only Philip, as his duty required, sent a strait faced note of congratulation. More typically, the Cardinal of Lorraine is alleged to have commented 'this time we shall not have so long to wait (for confirmation), as it is already eight months since her husband left her...' His arithmetic was defective, but his scepticism was generally shared. After the original announcement, there is an eyrie silence about this second 'pregnancy'. Whereas on the first occasion there had been much comment on the advancing symptoms, particularly the shape of the queen's body, this time nobody seems to have noticed. It would appear that Mary's condition existed only in her own mind, and that her physicians either would not, or could not, persuade her otherwise. The only possible conclusion was that she was ill, but how ill was not apparent. In the early part of 1558 the loss of Calais depressed her, and the fading prospect of a further visit from Philip, but no one commented on her distress at a further failed pregnancy. In defiance of the evidence, and even of natural probability, Mary continued to believe that she would have issue until the autumn of 1558, less than two months before her own death.

During the last year of her life, although the religious persecution continued, and the volume of exile protestant criticism continued to grow, opposition to Mary at home subsided.

This may have been because loyalty was revived by the war, or because her regime was developing a new stability on the assumption that Philip would play no further part. Or it may have been a 'waiting calm', based on nothing more positive than an assumption that her days were numbered and there was nothing to be gained by premature action. When Mary drew up her will early in 1558, it still spoke of issue 'of her body lawfully begotten', and it was only when she added a codicil in October that she admitted that such an event was uncertain. Although she is alleged to have said that Calais would be found written on her heart, the bitterest failure that Mary had to bear was dynastic. Although she may have thought that she had come to terms with celibacy when her marriage was so long delayed, when the opportunity finally presented itself she desperately wanted a child, for both personal and political reasons. She distrusted Elizabeth profoundly, and was well aware that Philip would press no claim to the succession in his own right. She also knew that her enemies would take advantage of her childlessness to claim that God had turned his back on her. Her faith did not waver under this affliction, any more than it had under the earlier ones, but it is not surprising that when she was dying she had visions of angels 'like little children'.


# VII
## War and the succession

One of the disadvantages of being a ruling queen was that you could not lead an army into battle. Elizabeth hated war, not only because it was expensive, but because it meant conceding authority to the men whose business it was to fight it. The bigger the war, the more important the commanders, and the greater the concessions which had to be made. Mary does not seem to have shared that view, and the many differences between the sisters are sharply highlighted by this. Mary had no doubts about her royal patrimony, or about the promptings of her conscience, but when it came to relations with her husband, conscience was an uncertain guide. Mary knew that as a wife she had a duty to obey, but she also knew that Philip did not always understand what it was reasonable to demand. As we have seen, she found it necessary to find excuses to avoid some of his more pressing requests. That was why war with France was such an important issue for her. Here she could do her duty both as a wife and as a queen, and it was no sacrifice to concede the leadership in war to a man to whom she was already committed. Mary never pretended that the war which broke out in 1557 was her conflict, and she made no attempt to project herself as a war leader, even in the female guise as an inspirer of heroic deeds. It is hard to imagine Mary making Elizabeth's Tilbury speech. Although her compliance gratified Philip as well as pacifying her own conscience, England's support did not amount to much in either military or financial terms, and the queen's relations with her own subjects benefited not at all. Part of the trouble was that Mary had no theatrical gifts, and her sexuality was basic and extremely private. As some of Philip's servants revealingly complained, she did not even know how to dress. She had a voracious appetite for expensive jewels and fabrics, but no sense of style and no instinct for self-presentation. Unlike her father, or her sister, she was incapable of a grand gesture.

After the siege of St.Quentin in August 1557, in which the English force played a minor but creditable part, the war was downhill all the way. England's last continental outpost, Calais, was thought to be impregnable, but the fortifications had not been repaired for about eight or nine years, and towards the end of 1557 the garrison was reduced as an economy measure. It was assumed that the campaigning season was over, but the Duke of Guise was in urgent need of a spectacular success to redeem his failures in Italy, and after a discreet investigation, decided that Calais was a soft target. It was Philip's spies who first detected that something was afoot, but the English council ignored his warnings until it was far too late. In a lightening strike early in January, Guise seized the fort of Rysbank, which controlled the entrance to the harbour. [28] Although English warships were already at sea, they were unable to enter, and the town fell within a few days. At first the small fort of Guisnes continued to hold out, and frantic attempts were made to mobilise a relief force; but the continuing influenza epidemic inhibited mustering, and the ships were scattered by a storm. Eventually nothing was done; Guisnes fell and the half-mobilised force was stood down. Philip himself said little, but his commanders were bitterly critical of what they saw as English spinelessness, and the English, with no real justification at all, blamed the king for not coming to the rescue. Philip's forces were in winter quarters when the alarm was raised, but he did send a small force, which arrived too late because of the speed of the English surrender. Scapegoats were needed, and the Imperialists soon remembered that Calais was full of heretics, who had undoubtedly betrayed the town out of malice. The English council was eager to concur, and when the Lieutenant, Lord Wentworth, emerged from a French prison, he found himself accused of treason. He had certainly showed a marked lack of resolution, but there is no evidence of anything more sinister, and the real culprit was the council, which had neglected the fortifications and run down the garrison. It should also be said that the Duke of Guise had shown exceptional skill and initiative, and well deserved the credit he received.

The only English involvement thereafter was at sea, and was moderately successful, apart from a disastrous raid on the Orkneys. More important than the actual fighting however, was the impact which the state of war had on England's military organisation. The country was divided into a number of military governorships under Lords Lieutenant. In some cases these lieutenancies covered only a single county, but the normal arrangement was to group counties together. The lieutenants appointed were nearly always noblemen resident in the area concerned, and the idea seems to have been a partial resurrection of the noble affinity, but under the control of the council. Each lieutenant was to be assisted by a team of Deputy Lieutenants, who were the Justices of the Peace wearing military hats. The idea was not entirely new. Henry VIII had used regional Lieutenants in special circumstances, and Northumberland had also made a few such appointments, but as a system Mary's arrangement was an innovation. Mary was the only Tudor not to be profoundly suspicious of the military pretensions of the older nobility. She had already restored the ancient houses of Howard and Courtenay, and in May 1557 she recreated the Earldom of Northumberland for Sir Thomas Percy. This was clearly done to strengthen the defences of the northern borders, as war with France always involved hostilities with the Scots, but it is significant that Mary chose to do it in this way. The parliament which met in January 1558 also passed two statutes redefining the military obligations of male citizens, and the weapons with which they were supposed to provide themselves. [29] These statutes remained the basis of the militia organisation until the introduction of county armouries, late in Elizabeth's reign.

In the event, very few Englishmen were actually involved in the fighting. The force which Pembroke took to St.Quentin numbered about 10,000, but it served for less than three months; and there were no hostilities on the northern marches, beyond routine skirmishing. The main impact of the war on England was financial. In spite of the fact that Philip paid for the expeditionary force, the Crown debt rose inexorably during the last eighteen months of the reign. In the spring of 1557 it had been reduced below the level which Mary had inherited, probably to about £150,000. By the time that she died that had more than doubled. Gresham, who served Mary as well as he had done Edward, managed to keep the repayments and recycling under control, so that English credit remained sound and the exchange rate stable, but the burden of servicing such a debt was considerable - and the country gained absolutely nothing by its efforts. In 1557 Mary resorted to the old fashioned and unpopular expedient of a Privy Seal loan. There was much grumbling, but no resistance, and £110,000 was collected. It was not until early in 1558 that she made a more orthodox and acceptable approach to parliament for a war subsidy. This was granted without much debate, but scheduled over such a long period that its value was much reduced. As we have seen, Philip's interventions in matters of trade had strained relations with the City of London; so much so that a request for a loan of £10,000 had at one point been refused. However, neither side could afford a serious breakdown, and the Merchant Adventurers reluctantly agreed to broker the queen's debts, using their cloth credits as cover. It was this co-operation which enabled Gresham to keep the loan repayments under control. Mary's only interest in commerce was to try and persuade her merchants not to upset Philip, which was one reason why she was happy to charter the Muscovy Company in 1555. This was a significant step in expanding the City's commercial horizons; and the king had not the slightest interest in Russia.

By the summer of 1558 both the main protagonists in the war were feeling the strain, and looking for a way out. England was marking time. The queen was not obviously ill, but was dispirited and lacking the energy for any new initiatives. Her experienced senior secretary, Sir William Petre, had retired in somewhat mysterious circumstance and been replaced by the undistinguished John Boxall. Cardinal Pole was similarly lacking in animation; in March 1558 one of Philip's servants described him as 'a dead man'. Paul IV had been frustrated in his bid to send another Legate to England, but remained deeply hostile to the Archbishop of Canterbury. Pole's friends in Rome were in prison on various charges, and nothing could be achieved. English sees remained unfilled, and there were six vacancies by the autumn of 1558. Only the persecution went on, increasingly mechanical and pointless. Even the exemplary purpose had been abandoned, and executions were conducted early in the morning to avoid attracting hostile crowds. To the historian, aware of what was to happen next, all this looks extremely *fin de siecle*, but it was not necessarily so. Paul IV was a very old man, and could have died at any time. A change of attitude in Rome could have breathed new life into the English mission. Had that happened, and the war been brought to an end, Mary's own spirits might have recovered. She would have remained childless, and Philip would soon have ceased to be a factor, one way or another, but Mary might have reigned for many more years.

Would that have changed the whole course of English history, and left her as the ruler who restored normality after the aberrations of her father and brother? There are reasons to doubt that. The protestants had not been defeated, and their publicists had become increasingly radical, abandoning their former non-resistance principles. Writers such as John Ponet and Christopher Goodman were appealing openly to the aristocracy of England to do their duty and remove the idolater who was so offensive to God. [30] That in itself might not have mattered; actions do not necessarily follow words. However, circumstances had also presented the English protestants with the opportunity to be patriots, resisting foreign oppression. If Philip had been forced to abandoned his wife, that position might have lost much of its appeal, but at the same time his power would no longer have been available to provide support. More seriously, there was a good deal of ambivalence towards the regime. However popular the old faith may have been, the papacy was not; and nothing in recent experience had altered that - if anything it had reinforced it. Mary had also appeared incapable of pursiung an independent policy in English interests. Even if Philip was no longer her husband, would she have been willing to cut her Hapbsburg ties completely and follow the priorities which her subjects wanted? Above all, would she have been able, on her own, to outface the appeal of her younger and much more charismatic sister? Mary's more committed supporters had feared Elizabeth from the beginning. Renard had wanted her executed; Philip had wanted her safely married out of the country. Her supporters were as discreet as she was herself, and it is very hard to discover how numerous they were, or how strongly committed. It is probably safe to say that if she had challenged Mary before July 1555, she would have lost; and after that, there was less need. She was seventeen years younger than her sister, and in much better health. Once it was clear that Mary would have no child, time was on her side; and her position became even stronger when Mary failed to find an alternative heir with even the remotest chance of being accepted. Questions of what might have happened cannot be answered. The point of asking them is to form some opinion about how strongly supported Mary was during her lifetime. No significant body of opinion in England urged Elizabeth to maintain the Spanish alliance by accepting Philip's dutiful offer of marriage. Philip had been reluctantly accepted as King, because that was the queen's wish. Hardly anyone believed that he had been a good king, or that his power (such as it was) should be continued. More interestingly, there was no catholic party in the parliament of 1559. Mary's surviving bishops unanimously rejected Elizabeth's proposed settlement, but they had very little support. Most members of the Lords and Commons would probably have preferred the Henrician arrangement, but for a variety of reasons that was not on offer. Faced with a choice between Mary's *status quo* and a return to Edwardian protestantism, they accepted the latter. This did not mean that they were all protestants, but it did mean that they wanted a return to national independence and priorities. Although eventually it was to be Mary's religious intolerance which was most responsible for her unsavoury reputation, it was her failure to embrace national priorities which casts the greatest doubt upon the ability of her regime to survive in the long term.

Mary had nothing like her sister's ability to choose able servants. She inherited some good men, but promoted almost none. Nearly all those who were to enjoy such distinguished careers in the 1560s and 1570s lurked in the shadow of Mary's disfavour, without being in any way involved in treasonable activity. Elizabeth's long reign, and relative success, consigned her sister to the historical scrap heap, but Mary's failure began in her own lifetime. She was not responsible for the childlessness which was her decisive misfortune, but her conscience deprived her of all sensitivity to the pragmatic winds of political advantage, and left her achievements without even such roots as they could have acquired in a short time. Mary's positive legacy was almost entirely unintentional as far as she was concerned. She left her navy in good order, an enhanced military structure, and a council well organised for its executive functions. Above all, she preserved the newly established

24

authority of Statute. In establishing her right to the throne; in repealing her brother's and her father's religious legislation; and eventually in recognising Elizabeth as her heir, she followed the precedents established in her father's reign, and confirmed his achievements. It is, however, very doubtful that she would have wished to be remembered for that.

## Notes:

1. *Acts and Monuments* (1583), 2098.
2. His mother, Elizabeth of York, was entirely English. His paternal grandmother, Margaret Beaufort, was also English. His paternal grandfather, Edmund Tudor, was half Welsh and half French.
3. The Salic law, so called because it was supposed to have originated with the Salian Franks, was an inheritance custom of the French Crown which forbade a woman either to inherit or to tansmit a claim.
4. *De Institutione Foeminae Christianae* (The Rearing of a Christian Woman) (1523)
5. A view of her expenses from 19th December 1533 to 30th September 1534 shows an income of £3000 (over about nine months) and an expenditure of £2950. This would have ranked her among the wealthiest peers. *Letters and Papers of the Reign of Henry VIII*, vii, 1208.
6. Statute 35 Henry VIII, c.1.
7. John Dudley, who had been created Earl of Warwick at the beginning of Edward's reign, led the coup which overthrew the Duke of Somerset in October 1549. He never took the title of Protector, but styled himself President of the Council.
8. Mary Stewart (Queen of Scotland in her own right since 1542) was the only child of James V and Mary of Guise. James V was the son of James IV and Margaret, Henry VIII's elder sister.
9. The surviving document is Harleian MS 35, f.364, in the British Library. It is described as a 'True coppie...taken out of the original under the Great Seal'; but there is no trace of it in the Patent Roll. It was printed by J.G. Nichols as an appendix to his edition of *The Chronicle of Queen Jane* (Camden Society, 1850).
10. The Imperial ambassadors were particularly bemused, because Mary's supporters had not been led by any great nobleman. They described England as 'populaire', and belived it to be chronically unstable.
11. Antoine de Perrenot, Bishop of Arras, was the son of Charles's former Chancellor, Nicholas de Perrenot. During the Emperor's frequent illnesses he managed international business mainly in consultation with Charles's sister, Mary of Hungary, who was Regent of the Low Countries. The Emperor still made decisions, but Arras decised how they were to be carried out.
12. Edward Courtenay was the son of Henry Courtenay, Marquis of Exeter, who had been attainted and executed in 1538; he was consequently the grandson of Catherine, a younger daughter of Edward IV. He had been brought up in prison, and in spite of a good education, had no idea how to conduct himself in the real world.
13. There was a remote dynastic connection, through John of Gaunt's marriage to Constance of Castile. The daughter of that marriage wedded Henry of Castile, and thus a small proportion of Philip's ancestry was English. A genealogical tree making this point was printed in London in 1554.
14. This instrument was drawn up on the 4th January, and copies were filed in a number of places in the royal archive. *Calendar of State Papers, Spanish*, xii, 4-6.
15. Statute 1 Mary, session 3, c.1.
16. A surprisingly large number remained secretly in London, protected by their English friends. A.

Pettegree, 'The Stranger Community in Marian London', in *Marian Protestantism; six studies* (1996).

17. Reginald's mother had been Margaret, Countess of Salisbury, the daughter of George, Duke of Clarence, younger brother of Edward IV.

18. Statute 1 & 2 Philip and Mary, c.8.

19. Mary executed more heretics in three and a half years than the Spanish Inquisition and the French Chambre Ardent together. John Foxe's *Acts and Monuments of the English Martyrs* (1563), which commemorated these deaths became one of the most influential books in the English language.

20. *La solenne et felice intrata delli serenissimi Re Philippo et Regina Maria d'Inghilterra* (Rome, 1555). *Viaje de Felipe II a Inglaterra* (Zaragoza, 1554). *The Copie of a letter sent into Scotland* (London, 1555). There were similar works in German and French.

21. Sydney Anglo, *Spectacle, Pageantry and Early Tudor Policy* (1965), 327-343.

22. This raid, led by Thomas Stafford, certainly made us of French ships, but it is by no means clear that they were provided by Henry II.

23. Margaret Douglas was the daughter of Margaret Tudor's second marriage, to Archibald Douglas, Earl of Angus. She was married to Matthew Stewart, Earl of Lennox, and was the mother of Henry, Lord Darnley.

24. D. Loades, *The Tudor Navy* (1992), 170-71.

25. D. Loades, *Two Tudor Conspiracies* (1965), 176-217.

26. G. Alexander, 'Bonner and the Marian persecutions', *History*, 60, 1975, 374-92.

27. Northumberland's eldest son, John, Earl of Warwick, had been released in October 1554 because of his poor health, and had died shortly after. Henry was to die in the course of the campaign.

28. This move was facilitated by the fact that the marshes which normally protected landward access to the fort, were frozen by exceptionally severe weather.

29. Statutes 4 & 5 Philip and Mary, cs.2, 3. 'An Acte for the having of horse armour and weapons' and 'An Acte for the taking of musters'.

30. Christopher Goodman, *How superior powers oght to be obeyd* (Geneva 1558); John Ponet, *A Shorte Treatise of Politike Power* (?Strasburgh 1556).

## Historiography and Bibliography

The only full study of the reign since that of J.A. Froude (reissued 1910) is my own (1991). There is, however, a brief survey by R. Tittler (1991) expressing a rather different point of view. There have also been good studies of specific aspects, notably by J.A. Muller (1926), E.H. Harbison (1940), J. Loach (1986) and A. Pettegree (1996). The relevant volumes of the Spanish Calendar were published in 1954, and the Domestic Calendar was issued in a new and much improved edition by C.S. Knighton in 1998. Interest in Philip as king has largely been confined to M. Rodriguez Salgado (1988), and articles by myself (1988) and G. Redworth (1997). The best of the old biographies of Mary is that of H.F.M. Prescott (1952). I have also published one more recently (1989) and there are popular studies by Carolly Erikson and Jasper Ridley.

## Select Sources
*Acts of the Privy Council*, ed. J.R. Dasent (London 1890-1907)
*Ambassades de Messieurs de Noailles en Angleterre*, ed. R.A. de Vertot (Leiden 1743)

Calendar of the Patent Rolls (London 1936-9)
Calendar of State Papers, Domestic, ed. C.S. Knighton (London 1998)
Calendar of State Papers, Spanish, ed. Royall Tyler et al. (London 1862-1954)
Calendar of State Papers, Venetian, ed Rawdon Brown et al. (London 1864-98)
Foxe, J., Acts and Monuments of Matters most speciall and memorable (London 1583)
Letters and Papers...of the Reign of Henry VIII, ed. J. Gairdner et al. (London 1862-1910)
D. MacCulloch, ed., 'The "Vita Mariae Angliae Reginae" of Robert Wingfield of Brantham'
        (Camden Miscellany, 28, 1984)
J.G. Nichols, ed., The Diary of Henry Machyn (Camden Society 1848)
J.G. Nichols, ed., The Chronicle of Queen Jane (Camden Society 1850, facsimile reprint, Felinfach
        1996)

**Further reading suggestions**
Adams, S., 'The Dudley clientele, 1553-1563', in The Tudor Nobility, ed. G. Bernard (Manchester
        1992)
Alexander, G., 'Bonner and the Marian persecution', History, 60, 1975
Alsop, J., 'The Act for the Queen's Regal Power, 1554', Parliamentary History, 13, 1994
Bartlett, K., The English exile community in Italy, & politial opposition to Mary I', Albion, 3, 1981
Carter, P., 'Mary Tudor, parliament, and the renunciation of first fruits, 1555', Historical Research,
        69, 1996
Crehan, J.H., 'The return to obedience; new judgement on Cardinal Pole', The Month, ns 14, 1955
Dietz, F.C., English Government Finance, 1485-1558 (Urbana, Illinois, 1921)
Duffy, E., 'Mary', in P. Marshall, ed., The Impact of the English Reformation, 1500-1640 (London
        1997)
Fenlon, D.B., Heresy and Obedience in Tridentine Italy (Cambridge 1972)
Frere, W.H., The Marian Reaction in its relation to the English clergy (London 1896)
Gammon, S.R., Statesman and Schemer; William, first Lord Paget, Tudor Minister (Newton
        Abbot 1973)
Glasgow, T., 'The navy in the French wars of Mary and Elizabeth, 1557-9', Mariners Mirror, 53,
        1967; and 54, 1968.
Graves, M.A.R., The House of Lords in the parliaments of Edward VI and Mary (Camb. 1981)
Harbison, E.H., Rival Ambassadors at the Court of Queen Mary (Princeton, NJ, 1940)
Hoak, D., 'Two revolutions in Tudor Government; the formation and organisation of Mary's Privy
        Council', in Revolution Reassessed, ed. C. Coleman and D. Starkey (London 1986)
Loach, J., 'Pamphlets and Politics, 1553-1558', Bulletin of the Institute of Historical Research, 48,
        1975
Loach, J., 'The Marian Establishment and the Printing Press', English Historical Review, 100, 1986
Loach, J., Parliament and the Crown in the reign of Mary Tudor (Oxford 1986)
Loach, J., and Tittler, R., The Mid-Tudor Polity, c.1540-1560 (London 1980)
Loades, D., Two Tudor Conspiracies (Cambridge 1965; Bangor 1991)
Loades, D., The Oxford Martyrs (London 1970; Bangor 1992)
Loades, D., The Reign of Mary Tudor (London 1991)
Loades, D., Mary Tudor; a life (Oxford 1989)
Loades, D., 'Philip II and the government of England' in Law and Government under the Tudors,
        ed. D. Loades, C.Cross and J. Scarisbrick (Cambridge 1988)
Martin, J.W., 'The protestant underground congregation of Mary's reign', Journal of Ecclesiastical
        History, 35, 1984.

Muller, J.A., *Stephen Gardiner and the Tudor Reaction* (London 1926)

Pettegree, A., *Marian Protestantism; six studies* (Aldershot 1996)

Pogson, R.H., 'Reginald Pole and the priorities of government in Mary Tudor's church', *Historical Journal*, 18, 1975

Prescott, H.F.M., *Mary Tudor* (London 1952)

Redworth, G., *In Defence of the Church Catholic; a life of Stephen Gardiner* (Oxford 1990)

Redworth, G., '"Matters impertinent to women"; male and female monarchy under Philip and Mary', *English Historical Review*, 112, 1997

Richards, J.M. `Mary Tudor as "sole Quene"? Gendering Tudor Monarchy, *Historical Journal 40, 1997*

Rodrîguez Salgado, M., *The Changing Face of Empire...1551-1559* (Cambridge 1988)

Tittler, R., *The Reign of Mary I* (London 1991)

Usher, B., '"In a time of persecution"; new light on the secret protestant congregation in Marian London', in *John Foxe and the English Reformation*, ed. D. Loades (Aldershot 1997)

Youngs, F.A., *The Proclamations of the Tudor Queens* (Cambridge 1976)